IGNITE YOUR MAGICAL PURPOSE

How To Feel Good, Make Magic, And Create A Rewarding Life

LENA ANANI

ISBN: 978-1-940847-80-1

Printed in the United States of America

DEDICATIONS

I dedicate this book to every single one of my clients.

I see you *Ignite Your Magical Purpose* daily,
reflecting back your soul's colorful essence
upon the communities you've created
and helped to live a better life.

You inspire me... every day.

CONTENTS

IGNITE YOUR MAGICAL PURPOSE

Congratulations on embracing your unique gifts and the desire to share them with the world. In using your gifts, you will discover that they can be used to help others, near and far. Luckily, your unique life experience has offered you everything you need to know to *Ignite Your Magical Purpose* and share it generously with the world. So, how will you do it?

If you don't yet know the answer, you've come to the right place. Like you, I also discovered my gifts and my voice. I am honored to share my words of wisdom with you, the same words of wisdom that I have shared with several others who, in-turn, became very successful in their own practices.

Whether you seek personal fulfillment or professional success, I will show you how to make your dream a reality.

With this concise, yet powerful, book you will discover the most important action steps that will get you closer to your goal. In this process you will also discover what holds you back from sharing your voice and how to conquer the roadblocks that prevent you from moving forward.

I know you will enjoy every ounce of delicious information provided in this book and I know you will walk away with several "aha" moments that will remain with you for a lifetime.

As soon as you experience your desired results, I invite you to share your success story with me by sending me an email to Success@YourMagicalPurpose.com with "My Success Story" in the subject line. I would absolutely love to hear about how you chose to *Ignite Your Magical Purpose*.

In the meantime, I wish you continued success along your inspired path. Thank you for reading my words and I truly hope they motivate you they way I have been motivated to share my voice with the world.

BE THE VOICE YOU WANT TO HEAR

Congratulations! You are actively and successfully being the change you want to see in the world. Everywhere I go, I see enlightened people like you making changes within themselves; believing it can be what changes the outcome of this world. More people are on the path of self-discovery; whether it's for personal or professional growth, people are beginning to make conscious decisions to adopt a successful lifestyle.

Now that you have been the living example of positive change, the question "what next?" arises. With all the self-awareness and self-improvement you have adopted, is there room to kick it up a notch and become a catalyst for the change you desire? Now that you have successfully applied a healthier mindset and made better choices, what can you do to invite others to do the same? What is your next step?

If you have ever found yourself asking these questions, then you are not alone. I too asked those same questions.

I wondered if I could find a way to share my voice with someone like you. I wondered if I could help improve your mindset. I wondered if I could lead you to have more positive and fulfilling life experiences. I wondered if I could inspire you to turn your dreams into realities.

So I asked myself, "How on earth could I do that?"

Should I entice you with visions of unlimited wealth? People who follow their purpose tend to find their wealth.

Should I lure you with visions of love and acceptance? People who follow their purpose tend to find the most amazing friendships and relationships.

Should I motivate you with visions of eternal happiness? People who follow their purpose tend to find joy in every moment of their life.

It would take more than the idea of wealth, love, and happiness to inspire you, because as good as that sounds, they are simply the byproducts of pursuing your magical purpose. I am living proof of that. Simply showing you what's on the other side would not be enough to get you there.

From my years of working with students and clients I learned that helping you discover the root cause of what is holding you back, and creating a system that works for you is the best way to get you closer to your dream. The tools I offer will change your mindset and the way you view the world, empowering you to *Ignite Your Magical Purpose*.

NO MORE EXCUSES

"I can't do it and here's why…" she says. My ears literally shut off after that point and I completely tune out. I know that sounds so mean, especially coming from a coach that has mentored many people to move past their limiting beliefs and excuses.

The truth is these excuses just agitate me, and they start to feel like poison taking over my body. If I don't switch off, then I could risk the possibility of adopting that person's fearful and negative mindset, which could potentially paralyze me and then my magical purpose would dissipate into nothingness. That's my biggest fear! To live a life without purpose or meaning. Yikes!

Meanwhile she is wrapping up her long convincing talk with herself. "So yeah that's why I don't think I'm ready to do it right now." That's when I tune back in and if I feel comfortable enough to call her out on her BS (and I usually am with most people), and then I simply move the discussion towards a place of "what ifs".

"Well, what if you could do it right now? What if you could afford it right now? What if you could make time for the one thing you've been desiring so badly to achieve?"

And then silence…

That's where the magic happens in conversations like this. Your power is in the positive what-ifs, not the negative ones. Your mindset is shifting from a place of creepy cobwebs to a place of shiny new realities when you allow yourself to consider what could really happen if you pursued the one thing you desire most.

For most of my clients, the one thing they desire most is to share their message with the world in a fun and authentic way. Come to think of it, me too!

If you were to ask them, "What if you could do it right now?" they would instantly perk up and shine brightly as they express from their soul how magical their life experience would be. That "what if" question works like a magic potion that can turn those poisonous excuses into prosperous manifestations.

I've come to a place in my life where I keep those low-vibrational excuse makers (aka Vampire Bullies) at an arm's length, because I have worked really hard to mold my mindset into one that empowers me in every area of my life, so I can continue to do the same for my clients.

To let others bring me down is not an option. Never.

I've turned away clients because of their inability to see past their excuses. Some people have managed to fuel their excuses into the most powerful mind and body paralyzer. Today, I can spot those people from a mile away. Ugh, just thinking of their long winded excuses makes my stomach turn. Tuning them out has been my saving grace, because it gives me an opportunity to help them see what life would be like if the excuses didn't exist.

Thankfully, my clients are people who feel comfortable sharing their challenges with me so that I can help them move past their roadblocks. Yes, they sometimes complain, but their minor complaints are being shared as a means to an end, the end being a successful outcome that we come up with together. They are receptive to implementing the tools I share with them to turn things around, and progress is achieved for the both of us. It's a win-win.

I bring this up, because I want to point out the difference between poisonous excuses and challenging roadblocks.

Excuses are like a black hole; you get lost in them. It's a poison that puts you under a spell, where you are stuck in a loop of words that continue to tell you why you can't make your life better. It's negative, dark, dreary, and lonely.

Roadblocks, on the other hand, have several ways to get around them. There's always a solution. When you share your roadblocks, you are opening yourself up to receiving a solution that you're most likely going to implement and use. You see the light at the end of the tunnel when you talk about your challenge. The possibilities of success exist.

Life sounds so much better when you shift your mindset from a place of "Here's why I can't" to a place of "What if I could? How would I do it?" The options are endless. And I know you can do whatever your heart and soul truly wants, so make some space in your life to create the room you need to *Ignite Your Magical Purpose*.

Ignite Your Magical Purpose by Lena Anani

LIVE AS COLORFUL AS YOU WANT

Many people fear being different. These people are followers, and allow their circle of friends and popular media to dictate what is "normal." They try to appear like the rest of their group. They find comfort in knowing that by being like everyone else, they won't stand out and feel awkward. Even if being, looking, and acting like the so called "norm" might be unhealthy for their mind and body, they believe that being unique might attract negative unwanted attention.

Being different is being authentic. When you move through the fear of being different you are saying "yes" to the creative soul inside of you. When you accept the idea of being different, you are spending less time and effort on hiding the real you. You open yourself up to creating a world that highlights your best qualities.

Which of the following statements resemble a thought you might have had in the past?

"Being different means that my peers will make fun of me, and worse, I might be shunned by my peers and will be left alone." – FRANK

"Being different means that I will stand out and receive more attention than my friends and would make them jealous and mean." – SALLY

Whether you share the same feelings as Frank (Fear of Failure) or Sally (Fear of Success), using the following visualization will help you move past your fear of being different whenever it creeps up on you. Use it once or as many times as you need to help you *Ignite Your Magical Purpose*.

Visualize yourself staring at a mirror. You see the person who has tried so hard to be like everyone else. Next to the mirror you see a treasure chest full of colorful hats, unique clothing, and a multitude of vibrant accessories. You reach into this treasure chest to pull out all the pieces that YOU want to wear, no matter how ridiculous you think you will look. Be creative, and pull out everything you want from this trunk and wear it. No one is judging you, so be as colorful as you want.

As you place the last item on yourself, look in the mirror and closely observe what you look like. Notice what colors you wore. Notice how you chose to wear them. Notice how completely unique you feel right now. You catch yourself smiling back at yourself in the mirror because you finally allowed yourself to be free and creative.

You suddenly notice whispers in the background and you notice they are coming from the room next door. Walk into that room. You find all your friends dressed creatively, too. Not one person in the room looks like any other. When your friends turn to notice you, they all cheer and applaud you for showing them that it's okay to be different and authentic.

This visualization works because it helps you move through the fear of failure and the fear of success that you carry from your fear of change. With this visualization, you now embrace being different as a positive experience and allow your mind to see all the good that can come from it.

SHAKE UP YOUR CHAKRAS

While the subject of Chakras is so large and sometimes complex enough to warrant its own book, because the knowledge out there on this topic is so extensive, I prefer to keep things simple to help you grasp the concept as quickly and easily as possible, and then encourage you to venture off and learn more about it on your own. With that said, let's begin!

Chakras are energy centers that reside inside and outside your ethereal body. We have more than we can count, both large and small. While we have several Chakras that extend down our arms, our hands, our feet, below our feet, and above our head, the ones we focus on the most as healers are known as the Seven Major Chakras.

The word Chakra, pronounced "sha-kra", originated in India. Chakra is a Hindi word that means balancing center, and in your Chakra research you'll find that there are Hindi symbols associated with each Chakra.

Healers mainly focus on the Seven Major Chakras because they are the power houses, our spiritual mitochondria, producing and processing energy that affect us on a daily basis. In my mind's eye, these healing centers look like faceted round gems of different sizes and colors. In your mind's eye, they could look completely different. Some see Chakras as spheres, like glowing balls of color, or funnel shaped, like miniature vortexes inside the body. All the Chakras are located in the center of your body along the invisible Chakra line from the top of your head to the base of your torso.

On the next page, I provide you with a quick and easy cheat-sheet describing each of the Seven Major Chakras to help you complete an effective Chakra Tune-Up.

Chakra	Color	Location	Key Words
1 - Base Chakra	Red	Base of the Spine	Grounding, Foundation, Survival, Security
2 - Sacral Chakra	Orange	2 inches below the navel	Sex, Money, Pleasure, Creativity
3 - Solar Plexus	Yellow	Mid-Torso	Personal Power, Will Power, Motivation
4 - Heart Chakra	Heart	Chest Area	Emotion, Love, Relationships, Healing
5 - Throat Chakra	Light Blue	Center of the Throat	Communication, Self-Expression
6 - Third Eye Chakra	Indigo Blue	Between Eye Brows	Mind's Eye, Wisdom, Clairvoyance
7 - Crown Chakra	Violet	Top of the head	Spiritual Connection, Energy Flow

To begin the Chakra Tune-Up, always start with the White Light meditation. As you inhale, pull in the White Light from the top of your head, your Crown Chakra. Allow the White Light to flood in and move through your Crown Chakra, down your Third Eye Chakra, down your Throat Chakra, down your Heart Chakra, and now disperse the White Light outwards through your shoulders, down your arms, and through your hands.

Next, take some time to tune into and assess each of your Chakras slowly.

How is your Base Chakra looking? Is it bright red and glowing with life, or is it dull and barely there? If it needs healing, breathe the White Light into your Base Chakra until you can see it glowing like a red ruby.

How is your Sacral Chakra looking? Is it bright orange and glowing with life, or is it dull and barely there? If it needs healing, breathe the White Light into your Base Chakra until you can see it glowing like citrine.

How is your Solar Plexus Chakra looking? Is it bright yellow and glowing with life, or is it dull and barely there? If it needs healing, breathe the White Light into your Base Chakra until you can see it glowing like a yellow diamond.

How is your Heart Chakra looking? Is it bright green and glowing with life, or is it dull and barely there? If it needs healing, breathe the White Light into your Base Chakra until you can see it glowing like an emerald.

How is your Throat Chakra looking? Is it bright blue and glowing with life, or is it dull and barely there? If it needs healing, breathe the White Light into your Base Chakra until you can see it glowing like a blue topaz.

How is your Third Eye Chakra looking? Is it bright indigo and glowing with life, or is it dull and barely there? If it needs healing, breathe the White Light into your Base Chakra until you can see it glowing like a blue sapphire.

How is your Crown Chakra looking? Is it bright violet and glowing with life, or is it dull and barely there? If it needs healing, breathe the White Light into your Base Chakra until you can see it glowing like an amethyst.

Once you've connected with all the Seven Major Chakras, allow the White Light to permeate and flow through each of the Chakras, starting with the Crown all the way down to the Base, making sure that the White Light can travel upwards and downwards through each Chakra.

Aligning your Chakras to the highest vibration of light and love makes opens you up to easily *Ignite Your Magical Purpose*.

BECOME FRIENDS WITH KARMA

How do you show up in the world? What kind of energy investments are you putting out there? Do you take stock of the ROI on your energy output? Have you noticed how what comes to you (or happens to you) is a direct reflection of what you are putting out into the world?

We humans gave this phenomena a really cool word to describe it: Karma. What is your relationship with Karma? Are you guys buddies or are you guys more like frenemies?

I encourage you to spend a few moments today to think about your relationship with Karma. Think about the crap in your life that you are dealing with right now, and how it might be linked to your attitudes, your thoughts, and your fears. Try not to blame this on other people or circumstances, just for now.

On the other side of the token, also think about all the awesomeness in your life that you are receiving in right now, and how it might be linked to your open heart, your generosity, and your unconditional love. Think about the ripple effect of good energy you've created for yourself and others.

Celebrate yourself for attracting all the good in your life. Honor yourself for re-framing your thoughts to heal the crap (life lessons) you've attracted in the past. You are a beautiful being of light and the power that resides inside of you is magnificent. Use your powers for good, always. Forgive yourself when you forget to do so. Become buddies with Karma and reap all the delicious benefits when you *Ignite Your Magical Purpose*.

Ignite Your Magical Purpose by Lena Anani

IGNITE YOUR INTUITIVE CANDLE

I strongly believe that everyone is intuitive. Your Intuition is most likely similar to a candle that hasn't been used or lit in awhile. So let's do this quick exercise to ignite your intuitive flame.

In your mind's eye, visualize a dusty candle. This is your intuitive candle. Use a feather duster to remove the layers of dust and cob webs. If your intuitive candle hasn't been used in a while, it's going to be somewhat filthy. So take your time cleaning it, removing layer after layer of dust, until you reveal a beautiful, shiny white candle. Pick up your candle, and blow your breath in the direction of the wick of your candle. With the breath of your Higher Self, you magically ignite your intuitive candle.

Your candle will last forever and does not melt away, but the flame may need to be re-ignited from time to time. Feel free to return to your intuitive candle and repeat this quick exercise whenever you feel you need to reignite your Intuition. Your candle will continue to light your intuitive path as long as you continue to use your Intuition.

Like I said earlier, you already have the gift of Intuition. We all do. It's just a matter of tapping into it, and then using it repeatedly, and trusting it more often. The more we act on our Intuition, the stronger our Intuition becomes. The more we gently tell Ego to step aside and allow our Higher Self to do the talking, the more Ego will begin to trust Higher Self; and Ego will eventually work in harmony with Higher Self.

Now let's assess your level of Intuition. On a scale of 1 to 10, how would you rate yourself on Intuition before you started reading this book? Next, rate yourself on Intuition at this point in the book. I know you've noticed a difference already. Most of the exercises we've done so far had you work simultaneously with energy while practicing your Intuition. Did you observe anything come up for your while you practiced some of the meditations or visualizations in this book? Everything you noticed was an example of you using your Intuition. This will just get better and better the more you practice.

To this day, I still receive emails from my clients -- months after giving them an intuitive reading -- where they validate my intuitive messages. Ego loves this, and makes Ego feel safe, allowing Higher Self to continue doing this type of work. The validation I have received gave me the confidence to write several books fueled by intuition, and teach several programs that create a ripple effect of love. Watching my students gain empowerment through my programs makes my heart sing.

When you rely more on your Intuition, you feel the same way, too. And you'll feel much more inclined to *Ignite Your Magical Purpose*.

JUST SAY NO TO VAMPIRE BULLIES

These days, we hear more and more stories on the news about bullies in our kid's schools, but rarely do we hear about the bullies in our adult life. Bullies are everywhere, and they come in all shapes, all sizes, and all ages. I like to call the adult form of bullies, Vampire Bullies, or better yet Vampbullies, because they just love to suck the life out of you.

How many times have you felt attacked by someone you work with or by one of your so-called friends? They use harsh and mean words to manipulate you to get what they want or to make you feel bad when they feel insecure about their "stuff". You know who they are, and you often find yourself wondering how you let them get away with it?

I blame fear. Yes, our good friend Fear, the one who is so great at keeping us alive and safe from lions and tigers and bears, oh my. But Fear has its faults. When it's not used solely for survival purposes, Fear steps in and clouds any spec of logical thinking or strong intuitive feelings about someone that just doesn't seem authentic. As adults, we actually choose who gets to mistreat us based on our fear of rejection, fear of being used, fear of betrayal, fear of physical pain, fear of emotional pain, fear of being alone, and so on.

Isn't it amazing how we let Fear control us? It's not even the fear that the Vampbully bestows upon us that has any power, but rather it's the fear within us that fuels the part of us that allows others to hurt us. So in essence we are actually bullying ourselves. You are as equally powerful as anyone else on this planet regardless of the extent of your human drama or circumstances. Because we are all created equally, we can say that it's up to us to decide whether or not we want to take the abuse any more.

A simple "no thank you" should make the Vampbully step aside and move on (remember, it's not your job to worry about who the bully will harass afterwards once you stand your ground). If they continue to attack you, then speak up, use your voice, and say your truth because regardless of the outcome (which you have no control of) you will still walk away feeling empowered because you were fully authentic in that moment.

Most likely, the Vampbully will move on and leave you alone, and when they do, say a silent loving prayer for them so that they may find the self-love they need to stop the cycle of abuse. Most of the time, Vampbullies are the way they are because they lack love, but I believe we can send them love (in the form of healing thoughts) without keeping them in our lives.

Take a moment now and think about at least one person in your life that you would classify as a Vampbully. Write or type a letter (don't worry I won't make you send it) and release everything pent up inside of you that you would like to say to that person. Then toss or delete the letter. Next, spend some time forgiving that person and send them love to heal the wounds they are carrying inside of them. And let's be grateful to the Vampbullies for offering us an opportunity to practice self-empowerment and unconditional love.

The more Vampbullies you release, the more energy you have to *Ignite Your Magical Purpose*.

THE SECRET SPICE OF LOVE

You know how your Grandma had a secret recipe for your favorite dish? No matter how hard you tried to get that recipe from her, she relentlessly said no time and time again. And yet you tried to recreate it on your own, and found it to be missing something -- that secret ingredient that you know you can place your finger on, but it's just not coming to you. And you ask your Mom if she ever saw your Grandma cooking that particular dish, and maybe caught a glimpse of that secret ingredient. But your Mom only remembers all the same ingredients that you already tried cooking with.

Well, it turns out that your Grandma's secret spice was unconditional love. She was simply cooking from the heart for the ones she loved. And you could easily taste the difference.

Unconditional love is such a power ingredient for anything we create. It amplifies the healing powers of food, hugs, thoughts, prayers, smiles, artwork, handmade gifts, and the list goes on. With that said, unconditional love also amplifies the energy healing experience. It takes your healing session with another person to a whole new level where healing occurs much faster and lasts longer.

It makes sense when you think about it. When we tune into Spirit to channel the light, we are tapping into the true source of unconditional love. And when we focus our own personal thoughts on unconditional love, we are exponentially increasing the power of that particular healing session.

I love sharing this exercise with my students because it really challenges them to break through barriers and to truly experience their inner power and inner healers.

The first step is easy. In your mind's eye, visualize Spirit hugging you, and feel that warm, unconditional loving embrace from your Creator. Know that you are just as divine as the One hugging you. Know that you are a loving, living being that receives love and sends love. Now take that unconditional love and visualize yourself hugging someone you love with that same light and love that you just received from Spirit. Choose someone with whom you have a very close and loving relationship with, someone you KNOW will receive it willingly. Note how wonderful that feels. Note how profound that feels. Note how you can actually feel your energy levels rising to a frequency of healing.

When I had my students perform this exercise, we all got a little light-headed because we collectively elevated the vibration of the room and everyone in it. It was that powerful. The healing levels in the room were so high that everyone experienced a shift!

If you are sending unconditional love, and it doesn't seem to be working for you, then try again. If you feel blocked or doubtful, gently tell your Ego to step aside. And always know that the other person will always receive what you have to offer.

I emphasize unconditional love, rather than just plain old regular love, because with unconditional love you let go of expectations. You release expectation from the other person; you release the expectation of yourself; and most importantly, you release the expectation of the outcome. You are thinking and feeling the following: "I love you so much, and I'm sending you love, and I don't expect anything in return." Without expectations, you are left with the purest form of love, straight from the source of divine healing.

Try once again to send unconditional love to someone you care about and notice the difference. Do you feel the shift of energy?

Do you feel it flow through you and into the person in your mind?

Higher Self loves that Soul-to-Soul connection, and most of the time will embrace the healing energy you send. That's why unconditional love is the secret ingredient to *Ignite Your Magical Purpose*.

Ignite Your Magical Purpose by Lena Anani

TRUST YOURSELF TO SHINE

Many people fear that they just don't know enough. These people are at times the eternal students that read every book and sign up for one class after another, without ever implementing what they learn. They find comfort in making plans to change the world as soon as they finish learning how to do so. They fear that they could never be perceived as the expert until they attain every possible credential. The fear of not knowing enough keeps their wisdom hidden from the world, prolonging the desired change they want to see.

By accepting that you do know enough to get you moving forward, you learn by leaps and bounds through your experience alone. It's an opportunity for you to apply what you already know in the real world, and let your audience teach you in return with their valuable feedback. When you move through the fear of not knowing enough you embrace and embody self-confidence and self-reliance. When you accept the idea that you already know what you need to know for this moment, you move closer with ease towards living your dream in action.

Which of the following statements resemble a thought you might have had in the past?

"People will just mock me if I pretend to be an expert at something without spending years in training. There's no way I can establish my credibility without it." – FRANK

"People are taking a huge risk if they believe what I have to share with them. There's no way I could possibly know everything I need to know to help others grow." – SALLY

Whether you share the same feelings as Frank (Fear of Failure) or Sally (Fear of Success), using the following visualization will help you move past your fear of not knowing enough whenever it creeps up on you. Use it once or as many times as you need to help you *Ignite Your Magical Purpose*.

Visualize yourself standing in front of five people. These five people look somewhat grey in color, wearing black and white clothing, and seem lost in sadness. You know you have what it takes to snap them out of it so you harness all the knowledge and wisdom you have collected to date and easily share it with those five people instantly with a snap of your fingers. Suddenly all five people are sitting up straight, full of color, and smiling from ear to ear.

Fast forward to a month from now, and find yourself standing in front of twenty-five people who are lost in sadness. With a snap of your fingers you share your healing wisdom plus everything you learned by experience in the last month. Just like the five people that you revived last month, you notice that the twenty-five people in front of you now are smiling from ear to ear.

Fast forward to a year from now, and find yourself standing in front of one hundred people who are lost in sadness. With a snap of your fingers, you share your healing wisdom plus everything you learned by experience in the last year and you revive another one hundred people.

This visualization works because it helps you move through the fear of failure and the fear of success that you carry from your fear of not knowing enough. With this visualization, you now embrace not knowing enough as a positive experience and allow your mind to see all the good that can come from it.

Ignite Your Magical Purpose by Lena Anani

PAY IT FORWARD

Earlier, I congratulated you for being the change you want to see in the world. Now, I congratulate you for stepping up and being the leader that this world desperately needs.

I congratulate you for acknowledging your fears and learning how to move through your fears. You are now ready to be the voice you want to hear in the world.

Always do your best instead of giving it the old college try. The word "trying" indicates a lazy attempt with the expectation of failure. To try something, you are already telling yourself that you might fail. To be the leader you are destined to be, you must commit to do it now. Remove the word "try" from your vocabulary. Choose to "do" or "do not".

Do not hold on to your gifts selfishly. Do not live as a student forever. Do not paralyze yourself with perfection. Do not be ashamed of your purpose. Do not allow others to tell you the extent of what you can and cannot do. Do not hide in the shadows of others. Do not underestimate what you have to offer. Do not hold back whatsoever because the message you hold inside could be the message that saves a life, or two, or a million.

Go out into the world and pursue your deepest passions with meaning and purpose. Fan that spark of fire inside to finally be the voice that your community needs to hear. Ignite your candle of confidence to kick-start your healing practice now. Accept that you no longer need the permission you seek to be the teacher that your students desperately need. Courageously create a ripple effect of love and light, and be the catalyst for world peace. This is your destiny.

My destiny is to share this message with you and to inspire you to pay it forward. Claim your power, claim your passion, and claim your purpose. Choose your path, share your message, and live your thrive in life. The time is now to *Ignite Your Magical Purpose*!

NOW LET'S DO THIS!

Wow! That was more information to take in that you expected, right? You don't need to master all of the tools I shared with you in this book. Instead, choose one to master and practice all of them daily in one small way.

Remember to take small steps. Yes you can dream big, please do. Small steps will ensure you reach the realization of your big dreams. One foot in front of the other. Small mindful steps in the direction of your dreams. Dream big. Write it down. Take action in small steps so you can celebrate and account for each small accomplishment. Small steps so you can easily commit to completing each one with joy. One foot in front of the other.

You can also reach out to me anytime for help or support with your goals. I've been coaching and mentoring clients for over 10 years now, and I absolutely love it! I've even helped several people start their own businesses, host their first workshops, and author their first books. It's such a rewarding life to live fully on purpose and to help other do it too!

So feel free to email me anytime with your questions at Support@YourMagicalPurpose.com and be sure to provide me with some details on how I can help you *Ignite Your Magical Purpose*.

With that I leave you with this final thought...

Shoot for the stars and wave to the moon as you fly by. Do not wait for perfection to appear before you decide to share your message with the world. Be the voice you want to hear in the world, and you will find that perfection already exists within you.

Ignite Your Magical Purpose, today and every day.

Ignite Your Magical Purpose by Lena Anani

ABOUT THE AUTHOR

Lena Anani is the passionate founder and creative alchemist of Your Magical Purpose™, a global community driven to experience life beyond the ordinary fulfilling their life's magical purpose. She joyfully serves her magical community as an Author, Teacher, Intuitive, and Mentor. She combines over a decade of experience from both her corporate path and a healing path, using her left-brain project management experience in conjunction with her right-brain creative healer experience. During her first few years of teaching, Lena was inspired to write her first book *Stop Look Listen: A Practical Guide to Intuitive Healing*, and later wrote her second book *OMG Do It Now: Be the Voice You Want to Hear in the World*.

She also coaches and mentors her clients by helping them design a successful authentic platform to motivate others as they share their magical purpose with the world. She has helped several inspired authors write and publish their first book, and continues to help many more authors devise a successful plan to launch their book through her very popular BrainstormYourBook.com program.

Lena's mission in her current lifetime is to enlighten and empower as many people as possible to create a ripple effect of unconditional love, and ultimately world peace.

You are invited to connect with Lena Anani anytime you want by emailing her at Support@YourMagicalPurpose.com with your questions, your comments, or just to say hi! ♥

* 9 7 8 1 9 4 0 8 4 7 8 0 1 *